Dear Teenage Girl

A collection of things I wish I could've told myself.

Katherine Kring

Copyright © 2019 Katherine Kring

All rights reserved.

ISBN-13: 9781791941024

I dedicate this book to my precious daughters, Eleanor & Finnley. You two are my inspiration and motivation for everything I do.

I love you.

Table of Contents

Forward 2
Chapter One 4
You deserve to have a voice.
Chapter Two 11
Taylor Swift totally gets me.
Chapter Three 16
What loving Jesus should actually look like.
Chapter Four 21
The purity movement let me down.
Chapter Five 28
I've messed up, too. Welcome to my Soap Box chapter.
Chapter Six 34
Boys sometimes suck.
Chapter Seven 41
I run weird.
Chapter Eight 46
We can't all be Victoria Secret models.
Chapter Nine 51
Social Media Detox Time.
Chapter Ten 56
Dear sixteen year old me.
A note to you 60
References 61

Katherine Kring

Forward

This book is a collection of things I wish I could've told myself around ten years ago. However, since I am not in the movie 'Back to the Future,' there's no way for me to do that. So I did the second best thing. I wrote a book and I'm sharing all my thoughts with you. My deepest hope and wish is for you to learn from my stories. Take note of my failures and remember my victories, so you can create an even more beautiful and courageous life for yourself.

I'm writing this for all the girls, emphasis on the *all*, please. This isn't just for the Christian girls, the goody girls, or the quiet girls. Of course, it's for those girls too. But it's also for the wild girls, the party girls, and the loud girls. It's for everyone, because I've tried to be all of those girls at some point or another in my life. I would be doing you a disservice if I didn't, at least, try to save you the trouble of having to be all the things you aren't. Can I let you in on a little secret? You can just be you. And be at peace with that. Don't let these growing years tear you apart and cause you to question who you are. Learn from me, laugh with me, and let's get through these tricky teen years together, shall we?

I would also like to offer a bit of a disclaimer. I am not an expert on any of these topics. I don't have a degree in psychology and I've never extensively studied the teenage brain. I actually have two degrees, one in Respiratory Science and another in Communication Arts. Neither of which have any real correlation to this book. However, I was at one time a teenage girl, just like you. I've been in your shoes and I would like to use my own personal experience as a guidebook, if you will, as you walk through this life.

Since I'm writing from personal experience, I made a point to be as open and transparent with you as possible. In doing so, I talk about some issues that may be a bit more PG-13 than a few mothers like. So, to give you a heads up now, I am going to discuss things like naked body image, sending inappropriate pictures through your phone, and having sex outside of marriage. My reasoning behind talking about such intimate and vulnerable topics (and for exposing my own secrets) is not to give permission or to shame anyone into thinking they are irredeemable, but on the contrary, I hope to display Jesus's grace, help you experience His forgiveness, and show you how to live in His love.

Katherine Kring

Chapter One

You deserve to have a voice.

When my siblings and I were growing up, my mom used to have us repeat the same mantra before we went out in public. She would say, "what are you kids going to act like?" and we would chime back, "little angels" and then she'd respond with, "and what are little angels?" and we would finish by saying, "seen and not heard!"

I honestly think my mother meant well when she started having us repeat this over and over again. She wanted us to behave, to not run around, and to sit still. As a mother, I can certainly see where she was coming from. I also want my two girls to not act like small monkeys in public. There's nothing worse than a toddler pitching a full on fit over cheerios when you're trying to grocery shop at Costco. However, as I grew up and entered my teenage years, I held onto that silly phrase from my childhood and it transformed into an unhealthy mentality.

Being seen and not heard turned into 'make yourself smaller, be quieter, and don't you dare stand out.' I wanted to blend in with everyone else. I was afraid to rock the boat or do anything that would offend someone. I was perfectly content being a follower because being a leader obviously meant I would have to be heard. There were so many times in high school that I wanted to take charge of a situation, whether that was in athletics or in the classroom. I knew the answer or I had a better way, but I was too trained or too afraid to speak up, so I just kept my ideas to myself. There were also many things I wanted to try, like running for class president or joining the volleyball team, but both of those things went against my ideals that I needed to be smaller. I needed to stay in the background. I could be seen by others, but certainly, not heard.

I can remember the day that I accidently let my invisibility shield down in English class. We were reading through Romeo and Juliet aloud and throughout class, my teacher, would ask us questions or have us explain what we thought was happening in a particular section of the book. I have always loved to read and it didn't matter if it was Junie B. Jones or George Orwell, I would devour it. My reading comprehension level was pretty stellar, so while some of my classmates struggled to grasp Shakespeare, I was enjoying every minute. (Side note, just to keep myself humble- I'm terrible at math. Like, almost failed algebra one, had to take college algebra twice, terrible. So there you go. We all have our kryptonite.) Anyway, as we were reading one afternoon, my teacher called on me to describe what was happening in the scene. He knew I understood the book, so I'm convinced he did this on purpose. Either he is a mean old man or a great teacher trying to unlock my hidden potential, the jury is still out. Of course, the scene just happened to be a little steamy and my cheeks instantly turned a shade of red that would have matched a clown's nose. After I successfully answered his question, he then made me go to the chalk board (yes, we still had a chalk board in our classroom) and write what was happening on the board. So there I was, a quiet, follower, easily embarrassed, teenage girl and I had to go up to the board and write in all capital letters, S-E-X. I thought I was going to pee myself, I was so mortified. My classmates all snickered at the word, but it felt like they were all laughing at me.

Unfortunately for my teacher, his tactics of breaking my quiet shell failed. Instead of feeling empowered that I understood Shakespeare, I retreated into myself more. I thought, 'if I just make myself smaller, then no one will notice me and call on me again.'

Friends, I could have enjoyed high school so much more had I not been afraid to be seen. I could've been a leader. I could've tried more. I may have failed more, or I may have even been embarrassed more, but at least I wouldn't have the regrets that I do now. Don't wait to be seen, like me. Show the world just how wonderful and insightful and brilliant you are. Raise your hand if you know the answer, talk to the new kid in the hall, try out for the thing that kind of scares you, it will all be worth it. I can promise you that.

In 1 Timothy 4:11 of the Message, the Apostle Paul writes, "...and don't let anyone put you down because you're young. Teach believers with your life: by word, by demeanor, by love, by faith, by integrity." [i]

Just because you're young, doesn't mean you can't make a difference in your own life or someone else's. It's never too early to start living a life of love and integrity. Just think of the ministry your life could have if you started at sixteen. Your impact would be boundless.

I think my biggest fear back then was what other people thought of me. If I raised my hand, if I shared my thoughts, if I stood up for someone else, would I be made fun of? Would I lose my friends? My mind was so wrapped up in what other people thought that I forgot to focus on what really mattered- what I thought of me. In Joshua 1:9 of the Message, it declares, "Haven't I commanded you? Strength! Courage! Don't be timid; don't get discouraged. God, your God, is with you every step of the way."[ii] How inspiring it is to know that our Heavenly Father wants us to be strong and courageous. Heck, He commands that of us. He created us to speak our minds and not remain quiet. And the best part is, He promises to be with us while we do it. Every step of the way, it says. No matter if we succeed or fail, He'll be there to stand by our side or pick us back up. You, my friend, are never alone.

I recently listened to a book called *Girl Wash Your Face by Rachel Hollis*. In this book she writes about one million brilliant things, but something that really stuck with me was the idea that "what other people think of you is none of your business."[iii] You aren't going to be able to change their opinion without changing yourself. And that is something you should never do. So instead of living in constant worry, give yourself permission to let that desire to please others go. Don't let anyone else have control over how you behave or think. The only person's opinion that should matter to you is Jesus'. And, friend, He already loves you unconditionally.

Unfortunately, it took me until my sophomore year of college to learn it was okay to be seen. It all started when I met a girl in my college math class that was always seen. She was loud and spunky and full of life. Her name was Melody, how fitting is that?! She knew everyone and it seemed like everyone knew her. One day, she leaned over while we were working on our assignments and cracked some joke about how bad she was at math. I laughed and confessed that I was equally bad, if not worse, than her. From that moment on, a friendship was born. One day we found ourselves both needing a roommate, the stars seemed to align, and I ended up living in an apartment with the loudest, craziest, most opposite of myself, girl I knew. We also had a third roommate, Morgan, who wasn't as wild as Mel, but defiantly more outgoing than me, so I guess you could say we all balanced each other out.

I suppose I could've gone my whole life trying to appease, be quiet, and keep life easy to handle at all times. I'm sure that would have been an alright existence. But what Mel showed me was that there is so much more to life than just existing. Did she take it a tad too far at times? Sure. Was she sometimes a bit obnoxious with her opinions? Of course. But it was all a part of who she was. She loved being the life of the party. She crushed it at being the center of attention. She was a leader in group projects, an initiator of plans, and she was always up for a healthy debate. As a follower, it was effortless to be around her. However, the longer I lived with her, the more I realized I didn't want to be a follower my whole life. But I didn't want to be Mel either. I don't think we should aspire to be exactly like anyone else. That person already exists, why would the world need two of them? I did envy how thrilling she made life seem, though. Throughout our time living together, I absorbed bits and pieces of how she lived her life and applied them to my own. That's how we shape ourselves into adulthood, isn't it? We gather up the tid-bits we've learned here and experiences we've shared there and we eventually form into who we were always meant to be. This process takes a long time. A lifetime, to be exact, but growing and learning new things is all a part of the journey, friends.

The exciting part is you don't have to wait until you're almost twenty years old to be seen. You can decide, right now, today, that you are going to be a leader. You can decide that you are going to try something new and step outside your comfort zone. I truly believe our world needs less comfort seekers and more people willing to take the leap. When we risk failure, we find the true reward. Our greatest reward is living a life worthy of what Jesus did for us. He didn't die on the cross so that we could sit on the sidelines of life and keep everything neat and simple. He died so we could live a full and abundant life and that means a messy one. Real life is full of ups and downs, wins and losses, where most things are messy and not just black and white. In John 10:10 of the Message, John writes that Jesus came so we could have "...real and eternal life, more and better life than they ever dreamed of."[iv] Life is much too short and our blessings are far too big to simply be invisible. Embrace the mess and let your light shine, dear one. The world needs to see you!

Chapter Two

Taylor Swift totally gets me.

I'm sure you've all heard the song, *"You Belong with Me" by Taylor Swift.* I would type out the lyrics here, but if I copy the lyrics down word for word, I'll get sued or something, so allow me to paraphrase. There's a part in the song where she talks about how the other girl wears short shorts and she wears t-shirts. The other girl is cheer captain, while she sits on the bleachers. If you don't know the song, take a moment, do yourself a favor, and YouTube it. And while you're at it, listen to the whole album because old T. Swift is my jam!

    In Jr. High, I was totally comfortable with who I was. I wore baggy clothes and no make-up. I had red hair (box dye, of course) and a wicked perm. I was a sight to behold, you guys. I was so comfortable in my own skin. I didn't care what anyone thought about me, because I thought I was awesome. If you watch the music video for *You Belong with Me*, I was band geek, T. Swift. And I was killing it.

I had a tight group of girls that I hung out with every day and I wrote in my diary about the cute rebellious boy I had a major crush on. I was basically living the teenage girl dream. But then high school started. My thoughts quickly went from, "I'm so awesome" to "Why am I different than everyone else?" I used to view that as good thing, but once I entered ninth grade it became more of an insecurity than a badge of honor. Now don't get me wrong, I still had friends that liked me for who I was- fake curly red hair and all. But, for some reason, that wasn't good enough anymore. I now felt like I needed to 'fit in'. Ugh, those dreaded words. I have grown to despise them for all the pain they've caused me.

As I entered my freshman year of high school, my only goal in life was to be popular. I had somehow gone from being nerd Taylor to desperately trying to be popular Taylor. Looking back, I'm sure I was a total drag to be around. I completely changed who I was. I started dressing more like the other girls and I even changed my hair. I remember not liking jeans from The Buckle, but you better believe I wore them after I saw the "cool girls" did. Bedazzled back pockets and all. I also didn't really like putting on make-up. I would much rather have a clean, fresh-feeling face. But you better believe I started wearing it every day. Because, duh, that's what popular girls did.

Not only did I try to change my appearance, but I also decided I needed to change my interests. I stuck with a few of my favorite extra-curricular activities for awhile; band and speech. But eventually I learned that those were 'way uncool' and I dropped them like a bad habit. With all my free time from dropping those activities, I decided to fix my gaze on a new challenge: Cheerleading. Friends, I HAD to be a cheerleader. Like, you don't even understand. It suddenly became my heart's desire. This was the epitome of popularity, in my mind.

Unfortunately for me, God had other plans, because, guess what? Freshmen year- didn't make the team. Sophomore year- didn't make the team. Junior year- didn't make the team. (It was almost like God was trying to tell me something...) However, persistence pays off, or not very many girls tried out. Whatever the reasoning, I made that dang cheer squad my senior year! I like to think that God finally said, "Alright, fine. Have it your way, but I warned you!" Although I certainly didn't realize or even think about it at the time, God was already before me. He knew the ending of this story. He knew that I was going to need him. But He allowed me to walk through that trial and He patiently and lovingly went alongside me. Deuteronomy 31:8 from the Message tells us, "...God is striding ahead of you. He is right there with you. He won't let you down; He won't leave you. Don't be intimidated. Don't worry."[v]

For transparency sake, I will honestly admit that being a cheerleader was fun. I really enjoyed being a part of a group. I think we all crave some kind of community whether we're in high school or our thirties. However, one of my greatest character flaws is aligning myself too closely with the community I find myself in. I tend to become whoever I'm around. In doing so, I end up losing myself. Teams or groups are great because of the differences. That's what creates challenges and leads to growth. When you eliminate the differences and act like whoever you're around, there is no growth. Quite the opposite- there is loss.

The problem during that time of my life was that I wasn't being authentic. I wasn't being my true self while I wore that uniform. It was almost like a costume to me. I put it on and transformed into this super confident, hyper, outgoing girl. But when the costume came off- I was none of those things. If anything, I was simply exhausted. It's tiring trying to be something you're not. Crowds have always made me anxious and constant loud noise gives me a headache. If in a large group of people, you can usually find me retreating to the back wall. That's just my personality. I thrive and come alive in small, quieter settings. Set me around a bonfire with five of my closest friends and I'll be the funniest girl you've ever met; but in front of a crowd- quiet as a church mouse.

So when these 'new friends' that I had gained from being a cheerleader got a glimpse into who I truly was, they wanted nothing to do with me. I wasn't living up to who I pretended to be. I wasn't the loud crazy girl they thought I was. I remember being told I was 'too pure' to hang out with them. Whatever that means. Looking back now, I feel bad for that version of myself. I tried so hard to fit in and be like the rest of the crowd and when I finally made it, they treated me like trash.

But you know what, friends? Those high school kids were wrong back then and they're still wrong today. It's never a bad thing to be yourself. Whatever personality traits God gave you are there for a reason. Instead of fighting against them, live into them. Be proud of who you are! Those traits are yours alone and when you fully embrace who you are, that is where the good stuff is. That's where you find peace and contentment.

When I was trying to be like someone else, I felt the opposite of fulfilled. I felt empty and lonely. It was a rough senior year for me. I didn't know who I was, which meant I didn't know what I stood for. So I ended up making bad decisions and constantly riding an emotional roller coaster. Rejection is a hard pill to swallow and it didn't go down easy. If I would have just stayed true to myself, I could've saved myself a lot of heartache from fake friends and ruthless boys.

I hope you girls will read this and realize how wonderful you are, just as you are. If you want to be a cheerleader, be one. If you want to sing in the choir, sing as loud and proud as you can. Just be authentic. Live into who God made you to be, regardless of what anyone else thinks or says. That is what it going to turn high school into some of the best years of your life.

Chapter Three

What loving Jesus should actually look like.

    If you were to ask my long time BFF, Bailee, what I was like in high school, I would bet she would use the phrase, "holier than thou." She would say this out of love, of course, but it would nonetheless be true. I took following the rules of the Bible to a whole new level. I was under the impression that if you wanted God to love you, you needed to obey every commandment perfectly, without exception. I was also under the impression that you couldn't be friends with people that didn't live by the same rules. This belief led me to appear rather entitled and rude to others. I never meant to come across that way, but my guilt from messing up every day (due to that whole not being perfect complex) caused me a lot of inner turmoil which when paired with fluctuating teenage hormones does not come out as the sweetest mixture. It literally pains me to type this, but I used to outright refuse to hang out with some people, because, in my mind, I was better than them.

Being the type-A, perfectionist that I am, I took having a relationship with God and kicked it up a notch. In doing so, I quickly turned a loving relationship with my Heavenly Father into a demanding and disappointing chain that I couldn't break loose from. It felt like Christianity had a chock hold on me. It was suffocating and impossible to keep up with this unrealistic standard I had set in my mind.

My faith and my attitude at the time stunk.

I was missing the biggest part of what it meant to walk with God. The part of the story that I apparently didn't understand was Jesus. As I mentioned earlier in the book, it's because of Him dying on the cross that we don't have to attempt perfection. Jesus gives us permission to fail, to be ourselves, and to have faith that we will still get to see God face to face someday. He took on the burden of our sins, so we could be freely forgiven. The sweetness of that grace is incomparable to anything else I've experienced. I only wish I could've understood Jesus and His love earlier because it would've drastically changed how I treated those around me.

As you can imagine, by the time I headed off to college, I was a bit burnt out on the whole God thing. Plus, I just gone through a rough senior year of not knowing who I was, so needless to say, I wasn't in the best place. None the less, I decided that as a good Christian girl, I needed to attend a Bible college. Little did I know, I would only attend for one semester.

I truthfully didn't know much about the place except that it was small and in Omaha, which were my only two requirements as I looked for schools. Going into college, I thought I was a pretty solid Christian, however, this place made me look like a rebel. And if you know me in real life- that's laughable.

This particular college had more rules than even I was accustomed to. The three that I hated the most were- curfew of 11:00 pm (I mean, come on! Don't we all go to college so we can have zero curfews?), no leggings as pants, and no dancing on campus. Right off the bat, I felt a little out of place there. Obviously, I was all about following the rules of the Bible, but I didn't remember reading any of those in the New Testament. Thou shall have a curfew even at the age of 19 was nowhere to be found in my Bible.

A couple months in, my suspicious feelings grew stronger when I had an RA tell me that I should only be friends with people that went to our college. I won't make a sweeping generalization here and say that everyone attending that school felt this way, but I knew after that conversation that this place was no longer for me.

You see, my attitude was slowly changing from holier than thou to accept everyone as I went through my first semester of classes. It was a requirement to take Old Testament, which meant a lot of studying and reading my Bible. As I was going through this class, the teacher often led us into the New

Testament and it was there that I started to get a better grasp on just how big of a deal this Jesus character was.

I ended up only staying at that college for a semester before transferring out. That environment may suit some people very well, but for me, as my faith grew, so did my outlook on life and I no longer felt like Jesus wanted me to only hang out with those who held the same beliefs. I realized it wasn't about following every rule in some crazy attempt to earn God's love. It was about how we treated others, how we treated ourselves, and most importantly, how well we understood God's grace and forgiveness.

I had a total light bulb moment in my apartment off 72nd street that year. Life as a follower of Jesus didn't have to be mundane or rigid. It was because of Jesus that life could be full of beauty and joy. Jesus died for us while we were still sinners. He took on that burden so we don't have to. Does that give us a free pass to sin as many times as we want with no consequences? Of course not. It means, He will love us through it. When we mess up and come crawling back, He will still be there with open arms. When you finally understand that and feel the radical freedom it brings you, your entire view of Christianity changes.

Throughout high school and that first semester of college, I thought I had to be perfect. And I thought I had to hang around other perfect people. However, perfection is unachievable. It's unrealistic. And the drive for it will only cause you to drive others away. Just like I did to my classmates in high school and just like that RA did to me in college.

Oh, and by the way, following Jesus doesn't have to make you a loser in high school; quite the contrary, actually. Following Jesus prompts you to love others, accept others, and hold no judgments. Acting like this will only attract more friends in the end. People want to be around people that are filled with joy, that make them feel comfortable and supported. We all crave that inner peace and contentment. You don't have to walk the halls of your school preaching the good news. Although, if you're into that, go for it. All you have to do is ask yourself the age old saying, 'What Would Jesus Do?' and then act accordingly. Would Jesus sit with the lonely kid at lunch? Yes. Would Jesus gossip about the new girl that just moved in? No. Would He ask her how she liked her new school? You better believe it, sister.

Sure, there will be haters. There always is. But those are the kids that need your love the most. I know it's hard and probably the last thing you want to do. Why should you have to show them kindness when all they do is bully you? You guessed it- because that's what Jesus would do. Hurting people tend to hurt people. Besides, you don't know what's really going on in their personal lives. Maybe they have an abusive parent or maybe they just experienced the death of a loved one or maybe they've never been shown love a day in their life. The reasoning doesn't matter. What matters is how you respond. Will you shut them out or invite them in? Eventually that goodness will break through whatever they're holding onto and Jesus will have a way to enter their hearts. And as they say in the Hokey Pokey, that's really what it's all about.

Chapter Four

The purity movement let me down.

Disclaimer: this is a more somber chapter. The topic is close to my heart. I take it rather seriously. We will joke and be light hearted after this one, I promise.

    I used to be terrified of sex. The thought of actually having to commit this action had me in cold sweats. Looking back, I blame the purity movement that swept our nation in the late nineties and early 2000's. I was convinced after this movement by the church that my purity ring would burst into flames if a guy even looked at me lustfully. I felt like God was a big bad monster in the sky that never wanted me to date. I'm sure whoever started that movement had awesome intentions about saving all youths from the evils of this world, but all it did was confuse me into thinking sex was shameful and my femininity was something to be embarrassed of.

The most confusing part, for me, was not knowing where the line of purity stood. Was I 'impure' if I held a boy's hand? Or how about kissing? Was that going to send me straight to the devil? I remember feeling so guilt ridden after my first kiss in the 7th grade. It was nothing to write home about friends, let me assure you of that. It was a quick peck from the guy I had been crushing on, in my yard, after track practice. But in my head, I was convinced that I had sinned against God and basically needed to attend confession and I'm not even Catholic. The confusion grew as I aged and by high school, my moral compass was all out of whack. The real bummer is, not only did that effect how I thought about sex, but it had a huge impact on how I thought about my own body.

For a long time, I thought my body was something to be ashamed of. I could hardly look at myself naked in a mirror. I remember thinking, if this is something that causes young men to 'fall' (as the church preached to me) then it must be bad. I better cover it all up. I don't want any of you to misunderstand me here, I'm a true believer in the old saying 'modest is hottest.' So, while I don't think you should EVER feel ashamed of your body or have any issues with your naked self, I'm also not indorsing walking around your neighborhood in all your glory. I believe life or relationships are more exciting if you leave a little something up to the imagination. My issue back then was that I took the "modest is hottest" saying a little too far. It lead to embarrassment of my body, instead of love for it. My lack of confidence and insecurity left me feeling awful about myself.

Let's set the standard now- Your body and your femininity are a gift from God. Period. And how do we handle a gift? We cherish it. We take care of it. We love it.

When God designed the first female, Eve, it was by no mistake that He gave her curves. He made her body different than Adam's on purpose. As girls, we should embrace these differences. Feel proud of our bodies. Feel strong in our bodies. It's not about overly flaunting our curves, so much so that others around us feel uncomfortable. But rather, simply feeling secure in our femininity. Because there is something so beautiful about a girl that is confident and at peace with who she is and how she looks.

The other reason the purity movement failed me was because it forgot to teach me about how amazing sex can be- inside the context of marriage. Sex was created by our loving Creator. It is for our enjoyment and also to make adorable babies someday. Where sex goes wrong is when you throw it around like confetti. This act is the most intimate and vulnerable part of life that you will ever experience. When girls and guys start treating it like a mundane, ordinary activity, it starts to lose its luster and that's where the long term ramifications enter the scene.

I honestly believe the beginning of your sex life will 100% shape how you view sex for the rest of your life. If you give away that gift too early or to the wrong guy, that drama is bound to follow you into the bedroom with your husband someday. You see, our hearts don't easily forget. We may forgive someone for how they've treated us, but our hearts hold on to those hurts, sometimes much longer than our heads. A friend of mine went through a very hard period of her life because of this tricky topic. She was in college at the time, but the story could easily be placed in high school. She had known this boy forever. They were friends at first, but through the years, that friendship grew into something more. She had such a soft place for him in her heart. And she truly believed he had the same for her. So she made the decision to have sex with this particular guy. All was well at first, but rather swiftly, the relationship changed from mutual love and respect to a booty call. The boy, whom she thought really liked her, treated her as if all she was worth was a late night text to come over. It seemed as though this had been his plan all along. He had gotten what he wanted out of her. Eventually, my friend saw through this act and put a stop to it. However, the damage had already been done to her sweet soul. I watched as this friend of mine struggled in future relationships to trust and fully give her heart away, afraid that she would be taken advantage of again. I know that may sound absolutely crazy to think about as a teenage girl, but that's how interwoven sex is into our souls and into who we are. I can't speak for guys because I'm obviously not one, but for a girl, sex is more emotional than physical. It has everything to do with feeling loved and accepted and treasured by another human being. So if you give that away and those feelings aren't reciprocated because some dumb boy decided to "hump & dump." How do you think you're going to view sex after that? Not well, my friends, not well.

That heart break will follow you around until you have the time and maturity to heal from it.

Don't just take my word for it. Let's look at what God says about sex. In 1 Corinthians 6:18-20 of The Message it is written, "There's more to sex than mere skin on skin. Sex is as much spiritual mystery as physical fact. As written in scripture, "the two become one." Since we want to become spiritually one with the Master, we must not pursue the kind of sex that avoids commitment and intimacy, leaving us more lonely than ever- the kind of sex that can never "become one." There is a sense in which sexual sins are different from all others. In sexual sin we violate the sacredness of our own bodies, these bodies that were made for God-given and God-modeled love, for "becoming one" with another..."[vi]

That was a huge chunk of scripture, so let's break it down. The first couple of verses speak to how special sex is. It is more than just skin to skin, it says. The author is saying that it's more than just a physical act. The Bible says the act of becoming one with your spouse is actually a spiritual mystery. I looked up mystery in the dictionary and according to Miriam Webster, mystery is defined as, "something not understood or beyond understanding." Sex is such a sacred act that our human brains cannot even 100% comprehend it. It's like faith or love or the wind. We know these things are real and we experience them, but yet, we have a hard time understanding or explaining them to others. It's just something we feel. Something that's there.

The next few lines talk about the consequences of pursuing sex outside of God's design. It says we will end up feeling lonelier than before. This is because when you have sex outside of marriage, it is devoid of commitment and intimacy. I know what you're thinking, you love that boy and he loves you, so that is commitment. So, I say this out of love to you, the commitment of a teenage boy or girl can be a very fickle thing. I hate to be the one to say it, but it's easy for a boyfriend to walk away. In fact, it's rarer when they don't. According to the Huffington Post, only 2% of high school sweethearts end up married.[vii] It's not impossible, but it's certainly not an everyday occurrence. I read a study once about the brain of a teenager. It basically said that our brains are run by pure emotions until our mid-twenties. There is no processing or logical reasoning going on, unless we pause long enough to take hold of our emotions. Our emotions can be powerful motivators. They can also change at the drop of a hat. Our hearts all ache for connection and commitment and it's very possible to have that in a relationship without sacrificing your one gift.

Finally, the last couple of lines get into how sexual sin is different than any other sin. This is because we are sinning against ourselves. I love how the writer uses the word violate because I think that the intensity of that word is so fundamental to this idea. When you give that gift away, you aren't only violating God's law, but you are violating your own body. You're hurting your own spirit, your own soul. I like to think of our souls as diamonds in the center of our bodies. When we do things like this, we take a pickaxe and we start to chip away. Each offense chips away a little more. What happens when you've finally broken away too much of the diamond? What happens when the cut runs too deep? The entire stone crumbles.

I know that these scars can heal and the diamond can rebuild itself. I've witnessed it. But like any scar, it never fully leaves us. That hurt in our past will always be around. Just like a scar on our skin never 100% disappears. And just as we guard an area we once hurt on our physical bodies, we will guard our hearts a bit closer too. Unfortunately, when we keep our guard up, it's harder to let the right person all the way in, to really let them see you, and know you. And, ultimately, to love you as you deserve to be loved.

At the end of the day, no one can make this choice for you. I'm not going to make you sign a purity pledge at the end of this book (like I had to do at fourteen) or guilt you into abstinence. I just don't believe in that one bit. The decision is purely yours. No amount of guilt will work if your heart isn't tugging you in that direction.

So I will simply close this chapter with this piece of advice:

Take care of your heart. Tend to it. Let God whisper His love into it and then listen to Him. That peace will guide you through any decision you have to make.

Chapter Five

I've messed up, too. Welcome to my Soap Box chapter.

    I don't want any of you to think that following Christ is always an easy road. I also don't want you to think that I've lived a perfect life and never messed up. I would be a total liar if I didn't tell you that there have been bumps, curves, and giant potholes that came out of nowhere throughout my life. And sometimes, okay most of the time, these bumps caused me to screw up. I didn't always hold my ground. I didn't always live up to the standard that was set before me. The hardest part to swallow was that no one forced me into those poor decisions. They were mine to make, just like they will be yours to make someday. But, the key to remember is that you **do** have a choice; right or wrong, good or bad. The decision is up to you.

One summer night in a friend's basement bathroom, I made the wrong choice.

I had this boyfriend. He was super cute, guys. Like, dangerously charming, kind of cute. I thought he was the neatest thing since sliced bread. And so did a lot of girls in our school, which really upped my street cred. After we'd been dating for a hot minute, he decided it was time to take our relationship to the next level. The next base, if you will. But since we weren't together that night, this had to be done (according to him) via text message. If you aren't picking up what I'm laying down, this boyfriend of mine asked me to send him a picture of myself with minimal clothing on. Of course, he didn't come right out and say he wanted a nude. Come on guys, we were only like fifteen. But he definitely wanted to see some goods. The kind of picture you don't show your parents. Are we all on the same page here?

This act went against everything I stood for. This was basically the exact opposite of what the "purity movement" had taught me. If I went through with this, my purity ring would surely burst into flames! I felt cornered. I felt confused. I wanted to send back a 'how dare you ask that of me' text, but I didn't want to seem uncool and end up dumped, so I tried to get out of it with every excuse I could think of. It's too dark down here, I don't want to wake anyone up, I'm at a friend's house, it's the middle of the night, etc. I was using every excuse I could think of to get out of this picture fiasco. But if there's one thing I've learned about guys in my time here on Earth, it's how persistent they can be. So there I was, to send or not to send, that was my question. Well, as you may have assumed already, I sent.

Shame and isolation instantly flooded my system. I felt dirtier than I ever had. I immediately felt self-conscious of my body and afraid of what he would say. I hated that I just done something I didn't believe in. I hated even more that I had let a boy talk me into something I didn't believe in. I knew it was wrong. I felt so alone. So isolated. My first thoughts were that I had no one to talk to about this. I couldn't tell my mom, are you kidding me? She'd take my phone away for the rest of my life! And I didn't want to tell my friends. What would they think of me? What if they hadn't done something like this before? Was I the first one? Were they going to judge me? My head was spinning in that basement bathroom. I remember dropping my cool flip phone to the tile floor, sitting on the toilet seat in my matching pajama set and having myself a good cry.

What had I done? Now this picture existed for all eternity. Or at least that's what my parents used to tell me: "Once something is out there, you can never take it back. The internet is a wild and scary place, Kaile." Was this picture of my young fifteen year old body going to end up on the internet? Who would all see it? Could I trust this boy with something so vulnerable? As it turned out, I shouldn't have.

A few short months later (which felt like an eternity in my mind) we broke up for one reason or another. Rumor has it, my picture found its way onto many a young man's phone through a magical thing called, group messaging. I still shudder at the thought.

It was my lowest low. My most vulnerable moment. And to this day, I still can't stand that I allowed myself to get taken there.

That's what gets me the most. The fact that I let go of control. I let some stupid boy persuade me into making a choice that I KNEW was wrong. I put my fear of losing his 'love' (HA) before my own knowledge of consequences. I was no dummy back then. I knew something like that could happen. Although in my mind, we were obviously going to be in love forever, get married, and have ten babies. Duh! But I knew taking that picture would only lead to bad things. What good could've come of that? Nothing is the answer to that question. I could've and should've told that boy that I wasn't comfortable with that and if he didn't like it, then he was free to leave. But instead, I allowed my integrity to walk out the door.

I want to share this story as a lesson learned the hard way for me in hopes that it will be an easy one for you. Learn from my mistakes, friends. Don't ever let someone, boy or girl, take away your choice. You each need to decide who you are, what you stand for, and where your line is. Your line doesn't have to be where mine was. It can be closer or farther away. We're all different and have our own set of boundaries. The point is to realize what you're comfortable with and what you aren't, what you stand for and against, to create a boundary and then you stick to it.

I guess I'll be the one to break it to you if you haven't already figured it out; life and love are, unfortunately, not always rainbows and cupcakes. Love can be a magical, beautiful thing when it's with the right guy. But it can also be a heartbreaking, devastating mess when it's with someone who doesn't respect your boundaries and ideals. That's why I believe it's vital to remember that there is such a thing as a 'healthy no.' You are allowed to say no. You don't have to justify it or back it up with any reasoning, other than, 'I'm not comfortable or okay with that.' Period. It took me a long time to realize I had that power. I used to think if I told someone no, especially in the context we're talking about here, and it hurt his feelings or made him upset, then I was in the wrong. I felt like I always had to say yes, so as to protect the other person's feelings. But then I learned a very important lesson. I am only responsible for myself. My own feelings. My own attitude. I am not responsible for making my friends happy, my husband happy, or my family members happy. I don't have control over their emotions or thoughts. (Although sometimes I wish I did) The only thing I have control over is myself. The only thing you can control is yourself. You can't make him love you. You can't make him understand you. And you certainly can't make him respect your boundaries. Life is pretty black and white in that department. Either he respects you or he doesn't. The rest is up to you. You need to respect yourself enough, respect your own 'no' enough, to stay true to your boundaries.

There's a guy out there that won't pressure you or criticize you. There's a guy out there that will be patient with you. He will have similar beliefs as you. He will look at the line you've drawn in the sand. The line that says, 'This is how far I'm willing to go and not an inch further' and he will willingly and lovingly move to the same side as you. That is love, ladies. That is what you wait for. And I promise you will find it.

Chapter Six

Boys sometimes suck.

I had my first love at the ripe age of sixteen. At least, I thought I was in love at the time. Looking back now, I chuckle at myself for even declaring that as love. Young, naïve Kaile had no clue what real love looked like or acted like.

He was basically my first real boyfriend. Like took me to the movies, made out in the back of his truck, and attended all high school dances together, boyfriend. And I was one smitten kitten. You would've thought he made the world turn on its axis just by breathing. I was planning our wedding and naming our future babies before we even addressed graduation invites.

So there I was, all young and in love. What could go wrong? Well...apparently a lot.

Now, don't burn your book yet, ladies. I'm not writing this to convince you not to date in high school. I'm all about dating. Heck, I'm all for falling in love! I just want you to hear my story, so you can avoid getting as wrapped up and lost in someone else as I did.

I believe it was my junior year of high school when it happened. We had been a couple since the 8th grade, with the exception of a few breaks here and there. I sincerely hope that you all read the word "break" in Ross's voice from the show *Friends*. If you haven't binge watched all ten seasons of *Friends* yet, you aren't living life properly. Finish this book, then commit your life to Netflix until you've seen them all. You'll thank me later.

But, I digress. I can still perfectly recall the night it happened. I was sitting in my room, in our little Nebraska town. It was a school night. My cell phone rang and I looked down to see my boyfriend's name come across my pink razor phone. This was 2009, folks, so no iPhone yet. I answered my phone while sitting cross legged on my bed. I instantly knew something was wrong. He sounded so distant on the phone. I asked him what was going on and he said he had just left his best friends' house, where they had talked about our relationship. My hands started to get clammy and my heart began to race. I already knew his best friend wasn't crazy about me. "What do you mean you talked about us?" I asked him. I'll never forget his reply, "Kaile, I think we're moving too fast. We're really young for this serious of a relationship. I think we should break up." That was it: short, simple, and to the point. He didn't beat around the bush or try to sugar coat it for me. All I could think to say back was, "ok..." and then he hung up. And I was left dumbfounded. Literally, I was speechless. And that's a rare occurrence for me. I felt numb. I didn't know if I was sad or mad or flabbergasted. It took my heart about ten minutes to catch up with my brain and then it was like the Hoover dam broke. I wept. Like, can't breathe, snot pouring from my nose, ugly cry. It was not a pretty sight, friends. My parents both ran up the stairs to see what was happening to their precious teen daughter. Between sobs, I tried to fill them in on what had just happened, but I'm sure it sounded more like a dying cow than actual words.

I cried all throughout the night. My heart was utterly broken. In my mind, we were getting married. He was my forever. He was my best friend. The two of us had made all sorts of plans for college and our future together. In an instant, those plans vanished.

Thankfully, my angel of a mother let me stay home from school the next day. I walked around the house like a zombie. I didn't know what to do with myself. But the following day, against my better judgement, my parents said I had to go back to school. They tried to convince me that life would go on and that being around my friends would help. Unfortunately, they were very wrong. I walked from classroom to classroom in a fog. I'm not even sure if I showered before school that day. I can assure you, I looked like a hot mess. You know when you don't want to see someone in the halls, you end up seeing them everywhere? It always seems to work out like that. Well that is exactly what happened all that week. Everywhere I turned, there he was. It was like I couldn't escape what happened. And that was exactly what I wanted- to escape.

About a week later, I found out from a mutual friend that he had actually been doing some shady things while we were dating. There were a few signs here and there that I should've picked up on. Hind sight is 20/20, of course. Random numbers texting him, deleting messages, hiding his phone, etc. But as I mentioned earlier, I was in love and so very naïve. He would cover things up with his smooth talking ways and I would melt like butter. So when the truth finally came out, my already broken heart, shattered into even tinier pieces.

I wish I could tell you all that I bounced right back. I wish I could say that I leaned into Jesus during that hard time and grew even stronger in my faith. But what actually happened was quite the opposite.

I fell into a deep pit of depression. I was angry. My thoughts were so dark. I snapped at my parents and yelled at my siblings. I hid in my room and listened to terrible early 2000's punk rock. Avril Lavigne totally understood me at that time. I wrote ugly things about people in my journal and I treated everyone around me like dirt. I didn't want to eat. I didn't want to shower. I just wanted to sleep all day. All I felt was anger: numbing, suffocating, anger.

It was around that time when my mom finally decided I needed to see a therapist. I don't know if it was a mother's intuition or perhaps she was reading my journal or maybe she was just so sick of my awful mood, but her timing was impeccable.

I started seeing a Christian counselor named Cindy, once a week. Sometimes my mom would go into the session with me and sometimes I would go alone. That period of my life was hard on my mom. She received the brunt of my anger, regrettably. I'd always heard that we hurt the ones we love the most and I can attest to that being true now.

I'd be a liar if I said it wasn't a long road back to peace for me and a long road to forgiveness from my family and friends. But through a lot of help from Cindy, what an angel she was for dealing with my melodramatic self, and a lot of talking to God, I eventually got there. It wasn't easy though. I remember sitting through entire hour long sessions and not saying a word. Maybe it was pride or perhaps my heart was so icy that it took awhile to thaw out. Whatever the reason, eventually, Jesus won.

Cindy helped me remember who I was before I became wrapped up in someone else. I had gotten so lost in 'us,' I basically had to relearn what made me happy instead of what made him happy. She also helped me see that I was never alone throughout the whole break up and the subsequent events after. God never left my side. He didn't abandon me like I felt my boyfriend had. He didn't think I was too much or too serious or too anything. God loved me in those darker moments and still loves me exactly as I am. The shortest verse in the bible is found in John 11:35, The Message translation says, "Now Jesus wept."[viii] I find that verse so comforting when I'm struggling. Jesus doesn't turn away from us when we're experiencing painful moments. He doesn't think we're being needy or dramatic or annoying. He feels what we feel. He weeps when we weep. He laughs when we laugh. When I was crying in my room, He was right there, broken hearted as well. However, He likely didn't cuss out my ex-boyfriend in His head, like I did.

What I've learned now is that God always has perfect timing. He sees the bigger picture when I can't. There's an old saying my dad frequently uses about not being able to see the forest because of all the trees. It means that we sometimes get so lost in the trees, the small or short-lived problems of our lives, that we lose sight of the bigger picture aka the entire forest.

Even though that breakup was painful, God had something better for me in mind. You might not see it at the time. Heck, I sure didn't. I thought God had said "screw you, Kaile. Enjoy your heart break." But, all along, He had a plan for me. Who knows where I'd be in life had that break up not occurred. I can't say for sure, but I'm almost certain I would not be writing this book. If this book helps just one girl in any way at all, then that past hurt was totally worth it.

In life, we need to go through things that aren't much fun. It's pretty plain and simple, like that. We need to feel the pain of loss and heartache. We need to learn to lean on Jesus when life throws us those unexpected curve balls. Because that's where we learn to appreciate all the beautiful things that He has blessed us with. Without hard times, we can't truly appreciate the good times. Without the rain, do we truly appreciate the beauty of the rainbow? Laugh at my corniness all you want, but you know it's true!

If you're going through one of those times right now friend, hear me when I say this: you will get through it. You will come out on the other end stronger than before. God loves you and is with you. Trust in His plan for your life, even when it makes no sense. I promise you, He will not disappoint.

Chapter Seven

I run weird.

There was a guy in my class that was the epitome of cool. Everyone wanted to be his friend, myself included. That was until he pointed out something that was "wrong" with me in the 4th grade. I was sitting at my desk, reading my library book, when I heard this particular boy chuckle. He was sitting directly across from me and watching my face rather intently. I looked at him with a quizzical expression and asked what was so funny. He proceeded to tell me, quite loudly, in front of our whole class mind you, that I looked weird when I read because I moved my lips. Until that moment, I had never noticed that I moved my lips while I read. I recently Googled why some people mouth the words they are reading and I learned that children that learned to read phonetically often do this. I won't bore you with the science-y reasoning behind it, but it's a totally normal and quite a common habit to have. It also helps readers comprehend and remember what they're reading. (So basically, what I'm saying is, I was a better reader than that kid. Boom!) But to that boy in my 4th grade class, it was comical. I'm 26 years old now and I still catch myself mouthing the words as I read and I always think back to that boy teasing me.

A few years later in the 7th grade, I was running the 12 minute mile in PE class. This was a requirement to pass PE in my old school. Fun fact for you: I almost failed PE one year because I hid in the locker room instead of heading down to the track. My bestie and I snuck off and bought donuts instead. I had to write a paper on the history of football as punishment and to ensure my passing of the class. But anyway, back to my story: so there I was, running with some of my friends, discussing what we would have for lunch, I'm sure. And the same boy from my previous story came up from behind me and started to laugh again. Without me even probing to find out what exactly was so hilarious about the 12 minute mile, he exclaimed to everyone in ear shot that "Kaile kicks her right leg out to the side when she runs. She looks like a duck." I was mortified. Everyone started to laugh and I wanted to crawl in a hole and die. To this day, I can still feel that red burning feeling of embarrassment creeping up my neck when I think about that afternoon. And you better believe I remember it every time I run.

These two examples may sound silly to you. I know there are far worse examples of embarrassment out there. But to me, they were humiliating. I think the memories and embarrassment have stuck with me throughout these years because that boy decided to pick on the two very things I enjoyed most at the time. Reading and running. I was and still am pretty good at both of these things. Granted, I'm not as fast as I was in the 7th grade. Thank you, puberty. But I'm even more of a veracious reader now.

Because I enjoyed these two things so much, it was especially painful when I allowed that silly boy to make me feel self-conscious. By caring what this popular kid thought, I allowed him to make me feel insecure about myself. I was giving him all the power. I could've stood up for myself in either of those situations and turned his negative statements into positive ones by saying something like, "mouthing words makes you a faster reader" or "perhaps I do look duck-ish, but I'm a fast duck that won the 400 meter dash last week." Holla! But did I say either of those things? No. Instead, I shrunk down into myself and wallowed in my self-pity.

When a bully is trying to tear us down, we should look internally and build ourselves right back up. Remind yourself what you're good at, what you love about yourself, and what others love about you. Remember who are you and be proud of that. At the end of the day, there is only one you. No one else can bring to the table what you can. So you should never be ashamed of how you do something or say something. Seek out the positives about yourself and then actually verbalize them out loud. It will feel sort of silly at first, but I promise it will instill you with much needed confidence. Maybe wait until you're not in public though. That might actually give someone a reason to laugh at you.

We should never allow someone else to dictate how we feel about ourselves. Especially when it comes to things we enjoy. If you enjoy knitting sweaters for cats, knit away, dear one. If you love to swim competitively, I pray you swim like a fish till the day the good Lord calls you home. Don't let anyone, friend or foe, make you feel inferior or less than for enjoying your life.

If I could go back, I would view myself through a lens of grace, instead of harsh judgement. I would go back and tell young Kaile that it's okay to move your lips while you read. Who cares what that one stupid boy thinks? You're an awesome reader. Or that it's fine to run differently than someone else. All that matters is that you enjoy running! Stick with it!

But I can't go back. I can only use those moments to try and help you. No matter how cool, how popular, or how cute that silly boy is: you are in charge of your feelings. You are in the driver seat of your emotions. You don't have to surrender control over and feel embarrassed if you don't want to. Shake it off, move on, and use that bullying instance as a pivotal moment in your life to becoming an even better version of yourself.

Just the other night, I was reading in my bed and out of the blue, my husband said, "I've never noticed before that you mouth the words as you read them." Great, I thought. Another person to tease me about this. "It's adorable," he added. And then he gave my hand a little squeeze and went back to scrolling on his phone. It was a tiny moment that he'll likely never remember. But, for me, it was huge. An insecurity that I had held onto for so long was now an adorable quirk that my husband admired. When it's all said and done, you can't change or decide how someone else is going to view you. What one person may see as strange, another finds endearing.

Jenna Kutcher, a blogger, photographer, and Instagram influencer, was once quoted saying, "take other peoples' opinions with a grain of salt, add pepper, noodles, some cheese, because mac and cheese matters more than what anyone thinks about you. The end."[ix] The opinion of that boy in my class didn't matter then and it doesn't matter now. If you can learn that truth, you can face anything.

I've said it before and I'll say it again, hurting people, hurt people. We don't know what other people are going through in their own lives. Does that make it okay for them to attack us? Absolutely not. But, as followers of Christ, or just good hearted people in general, we should give them the benefit of the doubt and extend grace and forgiveness. Maybe that boy back in my 4th grade classroom was having a rough time at home. I don't know what was going on in his life. I didn't ask. Perhaps I should have. Perhaps we should all take a beat when we find ourselves in these situations and ask ourselves what the other person is going through and then maybe, just maybe, we could extend the olive branch of empathy and actually get down to the core of the problem.

Or, you know, perhaps that person is just mean. Let's be honest, sometimes people suck.

Chapter Eight

We can't all be Victoria Secret models.

I've always been on the shorter side. I'm a solid 5'3", but I usually fib and say I'm 5'4" when they ask at the doctor's office. Having a shorter frame means there's less forgiveness when I start to pack on the pounds. It doesn't quite distribute equally. When I lose weight, the first to go are the ladies up top, if you know what I mean. But when I gain the weight back, does it return to the girls? Nope. It heads straight for my hips. Life is so unfair like that.

In high school, I was super self conscious of my weight. Granted, I was never really that heavy. But in my mind, I looked hideous. I didn't like the way my clothes pulled at certain places or that I couldn't fit into a size 0 in pants. What kind of goal is that anyway? At some point or another, I got it into my head that skinny meant a size zero. However, I was not a size zero. So, instead of working out and trying to shed the extra weight the old fashioned way, I decided to take the easy way out and try diet pills.

During that same summer of taking "magic pills," I was working at a mini putt-putt course in my hometown. By working, I mean, I just laid out in the sun all day and read books because no one ever came to this putt-putt course. That summer was the one before my senior year and as you may recall, I finally made the cheer squad that year. So as August rolled around, that meant it was time to start cheerleading practice. Since I had an open course and plenty of time to kill, the team would come to me and we'd practice out in the sun. Unbeknownst to me, when you mix diet pills, little water, a lot of heat and exercise, you end up with a passed out teenager. That's right: I fainted in front of everyone.

To be fair, I did lose some of the weight during that summer of pills and fainting, but as you can probably assume, I also felt miserable and jittery the whole time. Not to mention, I gained it all back once I got off the pills, due to it being mostly water weight. The real issue was, I wasn't making my body stronger or trying to be a healthier version of myself. I was trying to look like the models I saw in the Victoria Secret window display at the mall. And that comparison was ruining my health and stealing my joy.

Unfortunately, that fainting incident didn't change my mind-set and I kept living with unhealthy habits all the way through my freshmen year of college. I could never stick to a workout plan because that took too much effort, but I also didn't want to take those pills anymore because, well quite frankly, losing consciousness is not as much fun as it sounds. So the next best thing was to simply stop eating. Now, I wasn't totally crazy, I knew I had to put something in the stomach, but I figured if I ate as much as a small rabbit, then I would be okay. I remember living in my first apartment off 72nd street and only having a grapefruit for breakfast, a few egg whites for lunch, and popcorn with no butter or salt for dinner. It didn't take long for my roommates to notice and offer their unwelcomed advice. But at that point in my life, I wasn't in a good place to heed warnings. All I knew or cared about was that I was finally feeling skinny and I didn't care if I had migraines or felt weak and nauseous most of the day. At least I could finally fit into smaller pants, right?!

To be totally honest with you, it wasn't until I became pregnant that I was comfortable in my own skin and appreciated the body that God gave me. I hated the way I looked from age 14 to 22. But then something just clicked for me when I was large and in charge with my first daughter, Eleanor. I recall standing in front of my full body mirror, looking at this big round belly protruding from the rest of my body, and thinking to myself, "Our bodies are such a gift. This is absolutely beautiful and amazing." Please don't take that as me advocating for you all to get pregnant in high school. That's certainly not the case. I just wanted to share with you how long it took for me to feel comfortable in my own skin. It wasn't an overnight transformation. This is real life, folks. And changing how you view your body can take some time. I share this with you because I think it's important for you to know that we all struggle with the same feelings. What you're going through, during these teenage years, is normal. We've all felt these ways. We may come from different backgrounds or have different skin color or hair color, but what we go through during those trying teenage years, is all relatable.

My main problem back then was that I was comparing myself to an unrealistic expectation of what the female body should look like. Yes, those Victoria Secret models are very thin, but they're also not 5'3". They're also photo shopped and air brushed to perfection by the time we see their ads in window displays.

Hear me on this, friends: I don't want to take anything away from how hard those models work to have the bodies they do. I've actually looked into it and most of the models we see in the VS fashion show work out every day, TWICE a day. I couldn't even get myself to work out twice a week in high school. They deserve those bodies because they literally work their butts off to have them. But even if I worked out that often, I would still never look like that. You know why? Because we have different body types. We were made differently. They were made to wear beautiful clothing and walk a run way. I was made to wear leggings and oversized hoodies and type out my ramblings for you. We all find our calling eventually.

I'm short and curvy while they're tall and lanky. Some people have broad shoulders, while others have extremely high cheek bones. We were all created by God to look different. And different is good. Different is unique. This world needs your very own brand of beautiful. It needs, more than ever right now, for young girls to embrace their bodies and feel confident in their own skin. You don't need any magic pill to make yourself look radiant. You already are.

Girls, here's three things you can do to stay strong and feel confident. It's very simple. Are you ready? Drink enough water to flush out those toxins every day, exercise for at least 20 minutes a day, and eat real food that fuels you. You don't need any crash diets, crazy fads, or any other magic that the world tries to sell you. Those three simple ideas will radically change your body and mind.

We only have these one bodies. Don't trash yours like I did. Love it and care for it and it will treat you well for years to come.

Chapter Nine

Social Media Detox Time.

I recently went through a solid stage of hating Instagram. It lasted for about a year. I would scroll through my feed and feel worse and worse about myself and the life I was living. I think it started because I used to follow many 'influencers,' as most of us tend to do. I found myself comparing what they had or what they did to my own life. How come I didn't have that much money? How come my face still had acne? How come their lives were so perfect and they seemed to have it all together? I'm lucky if I shower and do my hair all in the same day.

There is one insta-famous person that I still can't bring myself to follow. Her feed makes me so ungrateful for my own life. She has everything a person could want. Her life seems absolutely flawless. Even after years of growth and self-awareness, I still have my comparison triggers and she's one of them. When people tell you that comparison is the thief of joy, they aren't lying. So, I simply don't follow her anymore. I know my triggers and I don't try to tempt myself.

I'm 100% sure if I ever met her in real life and we talked for more than five minutes, I would get a glimpse into her actual reality and I bet it would be shockingly similar to mine. Just like the rest of us, her life isn't perfect. Her hair gets greasy and her stomach bloats after eating excessive amounts of pasta. I mean, there's simply no way around these things, people. But on Instagram, she appears to have no qualms. And there inlays the problem with social media.

Those tiny squares paint an unrealistic picture. They show us everyone else's highlight reel. We get an outsiders view of all the amazing things that are happening in our friends' and sometimes complete strangers' lives. The issue is, we don't always get to see the behind the scenes footage. We miss the opportunity to peek inside these people's lives and witness what is really happening. If only we could peer inside their actual lives and see how many attempts it took to get that perfect selfie or that adorable boomerang. I bet we would see that these moments they're capturing are meticulously planned and set up.

I certainly don't mean to throw any shade on these insta-famous folks, by the way. There is inherently nothing wrong with what they're doing. Kudos to them for taking something free and turning it into a lucrative business. TBH, I'm a little jealous that my feed isn't as beautiful (or profitable). Not to mention, there are lots of influencers out there that DO show the real deal, behind the scenes, kind of things. They take selfies with no make-up or filters and they go live to show us their dog puked on the perfect white rug or that they accidently left the top of the blender off and fruit smoothie now covers their ceiling.

The solution to social media envy is very simple. It's us. It's in how we respond to their flawless pictures as we scroll. Are we instantly jealous of their frizz-free hair or are we happy that they finally found a cure to an aesthetic issue that ails us all? Do we get down on ourselves after seeing that they're on yet another vacation or does it motivate us to hustle harder? Instead of comparing ourselves to these influencers, let's make a promise to simply be happy for them, cheer them on, and let it remind us to take a moment and look at all the blessings we have in our own lives. Instead of drowning in envy, let's make a promise to realize that these are highlight reels and not their whole story. Let's also take a beat to focus on the fact that we should never compare our beginning to someone else's middle (*Rachel Hollis* coined that phrase.) We're all at different places in our lives and we're all traveling at different speeds. We have different goals and aspirations to reach for. Imitation is not always the purest form of flattery. So, be true to who you are and stop trying to reproduce what you see as you scroll. Her life is her own. You can try all you want to copy and paste what you see in someone else's story into your own, but your attempts will be futile. It's simply impossible. You have your own life to live. Your own story to tell.

While listening to a podcast by *Jenna Kutcher*, I learned a very valuable lesson. She taught me that I was in the driver seat of my socials. I am in charge, no one else. If I'm unhappy scrolling through Insta and I'm constantly finding myself comparing or thinking negatively, that is on me. It's not anyone else's problem to solve. *Jenna* suggests doing a social media detox when you're feeling this way. It's very easy to do. Just sit down on the couch and think of the top three to five things that define your life. What makes you happy? What lights you up? What motivates you to keep going? What makes you better? Now make a list. Write it down on actual real paper. Lists always work better when we go from brain to paper. Then click on the list of all the people you're following and begin your detox. One by one ask yourself, does this person align with my list? Am I bettering myself by looking at this? Does this person make me smile or feel stronger? If your answer is a negative one, guess what? It's time to unfollow and never look back. Ain't nobody got time for that. Go through and unfollow or unlike anyone that is triggering those negative feelings for you. Instagram, Snapchat, or Facebook should bring you joy when you scroll through, not anxiety. You shouldn't feel like you need to be better at this or buy that. Take control of your social media platforms and decide what brings you joy and what doesn't serve you any longer. You no longer have to sit on the sidelines and allow social media to lay claim to your happiness.

It will feel like a weight is lifted after you've finished detoxing your socials. The freedom is real. You can grow and learn as you scroll through all the things or you can feel miserable and find yourself buried in a pint of Ben & Jerry's. The choice is yours, my dear. Choose wisely.

Side note: you can still eat Ben & Jerry's after you finish your social media detox. Just maybe not the whole pint.

Chapter Ten

Dear sixteen year old me.

Before we come to the end of my book, I have a little project for each of you. I know, I know, homework is gross. But this is a good one. Hear me out! I want you to think hard about what you wish to accomplish in the next ten years. What do you want to achieve? Who do you see yourself surrounded by? What kind of girl do you want to become? What qualities do you want to embody? What aspects of personal growth are important to you? Are you kinder to strangers? More forgiving of those that hurt you? You get the idea. Give yourself some time to really ponder these questions and then write a letter to your future self. However old you will be in ten years is how you should title this letter. So for example, if you're sixteen now, write out, "Dear 26 year old me." Then let your heart pour onto those pages. Write out your dreams, your fears, your beliefs; anything you want for your future self. Don't overthink it, just word-vomit. That's how the best, purest, most sincere letters are written.

When you're done, pray over your letter and ask God to guide you as you walk through the next ten years. Then fold it up and tuck that precious letter to yourself away in a safe place. You're going to want to read that in ten years, believe me.

Now you have a plan, my friends. You have a written goal for yourself. You can be that woman. You are brave enough and strong enough. All you need is belief in yourself.

Since I can't go back in time and write this letter to myself at 26, I thought I would do the opposite and write a letter to my sixteen year old self. I hope it inspires you to write your own.

Dear sixteen year old me,

I'd like to start off my saying that you're absolutely beautiful just the way you are. I know that's your biggest insecurity right now. That ideal body you have in your mind is an unrealistic and unnecessary expectation. Let it go and embrace your body as it is. Besides, strong is the new skinny. So, instead of trying to be paper thin, try filling your body with real food, like from the ground, food. You know, like those green vegetables mom always wants you to eat. Get off your bum and run, lift, start Pilates, take a yoga class, do whatever feels good that day, but don't stop moving. Your future body will thank you.

On a separate note, I hate to be the bearer of bad news, but there is going to be some heartbreak in your future. The good news is, you don't have to let it define you. You are so much stronger than you think. You have such a capacity for love and there is nothing wrong with feeling as much as you do. Feel all the feelings. Love as hard as you can. There is never regret in that. Just remember to not get lost in someone else. You are already a whole person. Not a half, waiting for someone to complete you. Also, while living those heartbreaks, remember to be nice to mom. I know you think she's a giant pain right about now. But she is seriously your saving grace. I'd hate to give away the ending, so trust me on this one. You'll see what I mean soon enough. She is patient with you and loves you unconditionally. And that, my dear, is a rare and beautiful find.

As you're going through your last few years of high school, don't worry so much about trying to fit in. It may sound cliché, but you were actually born to stand out. Quit wasting time attempting to be like everyone else or trying to become what anyone else wants you to become. You are wonderfully you, just as you are. Your quirks and oddities are what make you unique. So, forget about the heavy makeup and bedazzled jeans. Let go of that incessant need to be popular. It's highly overrated anyway.

Moreover, never forget to speak up. Your voice deserves to be heard and you have brilliant ideas to offer this world. I know it's easier to fade into the background, but that's not where real life happens. Let your life be messy. That's where the good stuff is.

Feel the freedom offered by Jesus's love and grace. Because you will fail, that's not an option, it's a life requirement. But failing doesn't mean you give up or live in shame. Failure is an opportunity to experience grace. Offer that grace to yourself, and then you'll be able to offer it to others.

Most importantly, try not to overcomplicate Jesus. It's rather simple, really. Love God, Love People. The end. That's all He actually asks of us when you break down the Bible to its simplest form. Sure there are rules to follow and laws that shouldn't be broken, but when you focus on the love, the rest just seems to fall into place.

Lastly, take a deep breath, pull your shoulders back (your posture needs improvement), raise your head high and enter that high school with confidence and kindness. Include everyone. Look people in the eyes. Don't be afraid to speak your mind. Lean on Jesus when you feel small. Remember that you are smart, courageous, and worthy of love.

Xoxo,
26 year old you.

Katherine Kring

A note to you:

Friends, it has been an honor to share my story with each and every one of you. I call you friends so often during this book because that is how I truly feel about you. I have welcomed you with open arms into my life with this book and I pray it serves you well. My hope is that it reaches you where you are and helps form you into who you were always meant to be. My greatest prayer is that these words will make you laugh, cause you to think, and inspire you to grow. I can't thank you enough for reading my words. It means the whole wide world to me.

I hope you always remember that us, older girls, are rooting for you from the other side. We know it's hard. We remember the tears, the heartbreaks, and the emotional highs and lows. High school is tough. But it can also be full of laughter and joy. You get to decide how you are going to view your current circumstance. You can wallow or you can rise above. You have the choice, each day. You are strong enough to survive these four years. But not only will you survive, you're going to thrive, sweet girl.

References

---

[i] The Holy Bible, 1 Timothy, 4:11. Peterson, Eugene H. The Message. Colorado Springs, CO: NavPress, 2002. Print.

[ii] The Holy Bible, Joshua 1:9. Peterson, Eugene H. The Message. Colorado Springs, CO: NavPress, 2002. Print.

[iii] Hollis, Rachel. Girl, Wash Your Face: Stop Believing the Lies About Who You Are so You Can Become Who You Were Meant to Be. Nashville, Tennessee: Nelson Books, an imprint of Thomas Nelson, 2018.

[iv] The Holy Bible, John 10:10. Peterson, Eugene H. The Message. Colorado Springs, CO: NavPress, 2002. Print.

[v] The Holy Bible, Deuteronomy 31:8. Peterson, Eugene H. The Message. Colorado Springs, CO: NavPress, 2002. Print.

[vi] The Holy Bible, 1 Corinthians 6:18-20. Peterson, Eugene H. The Message. Colorado Springs, CO: NavPress, 2002. Print.

[vii] Manning, Evan. "Are High School Relationships Worth it?" Huffington Post, 29 Jan. 2013, www.huffingtonpost.com/evan-manning/are-high-school-relations_b_2206549.html. Accessed 4 Oct. 2018.

[viii] The Holy Bible, John 11:35. Peterson, Eugene H. The Message. Colorado Springs, CO: NavPress, 2002. Print.

[ix] Kutcher, Jenna. Inspirational quote. Instagram, 11 Nov. 2018, www.instagram.com/p/BqGS21Ph_zj/

Made in the USA
Columbia, SC
11 December 2019